$12.00 US

Part of the proceeds from the sale of this book go to the building of a college in the countryside of Kep, Cambodia.

After

After

POEMS | **by Chath pierSath**

ABINGDON SQUARE PUBLISHING
New York

After
is published by
Abingdon Square Publishing
463 West Street, Suite G122
New York, NY 10014 USA
www.abingdonsquarepublishing.com

ISBN 978-0-9823480-4-8
Library of Congress Control Number: 2009909760

First Printing: October 2009
Printed in the United States of America

Book Design: Abingdon Square Publishing

Cover Art: *Untitled* © 2006 Chath pierSath

Part of the proceeds from the sale of this book go to
the building of a college in the countryside of Kep, Cambodia.

PREFACE

After is a body of poems that has been written over the last ten years. It has gone through three revisions. Father Nazarin did the first revision. My friend, Rick Sawyer, who passed away at age 52, did the second, and Timothy Smith, an artist and teacher, with whom I met in Cambodia did this last revision.

I dedicate this book to them, Father, Rick and Timothy, and also to Doug Baulos, who had helped me with other poems I would like to publish in future volumes. Lastly, to my best friend and partner, Ken Nicewicz, the kindest and the most generous man I had ever known.

INTRODUCTION

Chath pierSath is a poet, painter, educator and human rights activist. When I met Chath in 1994 in Cambodia, the country was returning from genocide and civil war to civil society. Chath had returned to Cambodia to help rebuild his country.

For Chath, rebuilding his country, or working on human rights projects, is never separate from his art and poetry, through which he reclaimed himself, a whole self, from the devastation of the war he had experienced as a child. His paintings and poetry are acts of reclamation and the urgency of seeing and naming what has been discarded or lost comes through his artwork. In his portraits of Cambodian children, faces portray an emotional depth that illuminates both human suffering and the capacity for hope. Chath engenders his subjects with the dignity and compassion that they have often been denied in life but which remain their birthright as full human beings nonetheless. He understands that there are those in society who see the people he is drawn to paint—the poorest of the poor, the dispossessed—as marginal. For Chath they are radiant and beautiful children living in difficult circumstances who, like the lotus in Buddhist teachings, rise above the muddy water to open in the sun.

After is a collection of poems about freedom, peace, dignity, respect, and justice. As in his paintings, the poems are a testament to the resilience and creativity of the human spirit. His poems describe how war and violence destroy lives, tear families apart and fracture the human soul and, although they have grown out of the horrific circumstances of war, they inspire us by evoking possibilities for generosity, kindness and deep understanding.

After raises many questions. His poetry asks, "How can we bear witness to the truth of suffering and survival? How can we affirm life and at the same time bear witness to the suffering of humanity? How can we repair our injured world? What can we do?"

In recent history, artists and writers have responded to these questions raised by historical or political events to give the world enduring works of art and literature that protest injustice and defend human rights. They have claimed the right to speech itself and to the full spectrum of emotions and thoughts that make speech urgent and necessary. The specific events have passed, but the poetry of Anna Akhmatova, Francisco de Goya's *The Disasters of War,* and Picasso's *Guernica,* and others, still ignite in us a passion against injustice as well as the recognition of today's injured world and what there is left for us to do.

It is not surprising then that in times of uncertainty or change, or in times of personal, national or global trauma, we look to the artists and writers to help us understand the events and actions that confuse or terrify us. The poems in *After* speak to the events of war and will be recognizable to the many Cambodian people who have lived through the war and social violence. These poems also make it possible for readers to comprehend worlds and realities that lie beyond their personal experiences. Through Chath's poetry, young people in Cambodia, many of whom do not know about the Khmer Rouge, the civil war, the refugees, the internally displaced people, or the landmines, will gain access to a part of Cambodian history, and perhaps gain a new understanding of their families and their society. In these ways, Chath's poems are an important contribution to the Cambodian literature of testimony. Chath understands that self-expression is the core of self-empowerment through which he can breathe new energy into the practice of cultural democracy in Cambodia's changing society.

At the end of the civil war, Samdech Preah Maha Ghosananda, supreme Buddhist patriarch of Cambodian Buddhism and founder of the Dammaiyatra peace walks, returned to Cambodia to rebuild Buddhism and to teach peace and reconciliation. Asked how he could forgive the people who had murdered his entire family, he said he understood that loving one's oppressors might be difficult to do. He then added, "But it is the law of the universe that retaliation, hatred and revenge only continue the cycle."

Chath is a child of Maha Ghosananda, not in the biological sense, but certainly in a spiritual sense. Through his poetry he invites all of us to join him in a journey of love.

Valentina DuBasky
New York, 2009

CONTENTS

PROLOGUE

And the Americans bombed.

So many bombs that
Cambodians cried,
choking on their own blood.
Bodies of children
scattered about,
Flat earth turned
into bomb craters.
Cities wasted in flame.

So many bombs that
ravens and crows
became the people's
victors and heroes.

Year of the white flag
on the wings of those
crows and ravens
with beaks pulling triggers
against the bourgeois.

"The imperialists are bombing,"
they cawed.
"You must leave your village,
your city, your town."

"Take nothing."

"We'll be back in a few days."

April 17, 1975
came the Khmer Rouge
and the tyrannical host
of Angka.
And a few days
turned into
a three-year
hell on earth.

"Angka welcomes doctors,
nurses and teachers,
singers, writers, and poets.
Angka needs you,
the educated,
to help rebuild Cambodia!"

"Stand up!
Hurrah! Hurrah!
Democratic Kampuchea!"

But Angka, too, said:
"That person has
clean hands.
He doesn't look like
he has worked.
Capitalist!
Exploiter of the poor!
Kill him!"
"She wears glasses!
She must be an
intellectual.
Purge her!"

*   *   *   *   *

An earth full of
ant-like workers
marching about,
digging canals and lifting
heavy dirt on their shoulders.
In harsh heat and rain,
dragging feet through mud.
In hunger working tirelessly
for Angka,
for Death.

Marching against music.
Marching against education.
Marching against culture.

Mothers and fathers
killed,
and sentimental love
denounced.
Tears were forbidden,
emotion was a crime.

Laughter was discouraged.
Killing was routine.
And anyone who dared protest,
Died.

Cracking skulls replaced
the sounds of birds chirping,
and screams haunted the night.
Bodies came floating
on rivers and streams.

Disappearances meant dead.

Starvation was expected.

No past

    No present

        Year zero.

There was only
Angka.

A LETTER TO MY MOTHER

My eyes, mother,
are much like yours,
wilted, full of tears.
My hands flail
fighting death in my dreams.
My complexion's clay blood,
and my face aims for the sky,
with the hope that one day
I will understand
the ways of the world.

I see you in the distance,
one foot wounded,
limping home on an empty dirt road
looking for your children.
The Khmer Rouge had taken them
taken them
to Angka's slave labor.
For three years there was no news.

The one son remaining,
I watched you search for answers
about a war
you could not win.
Like other mothers
you tried to battle it,
your intention to save
what was left of your children.

With no rice for our plates,

you shaking with fever,
my two-year-old sister
swelling from starvation,
I went begging and gathering
to keep you both breathing.

I remember you calling my name
while I sat in a tree
eating leaves
to delay starvation.
I tried begging for rice
but the men who were eating
did not care.
They turned their backs
and laughed.

And I stood watching them.

I wanted to stay in that tree
among foliage rotten from suffering,
but your assurance,
your fine, thin hands stretching
peeled me down
from my hungry embrace.
Like the tree receiving
sun and rain for sustenance,
I took your words and tears
as my food.
But I so feared, mother
when you became gaunt and frail,
that you would leave me
orphaned in that mad country.

You lived to see
the return of your missing children.
Though on the torture list
of the Khmer Rouge,
the Vietnamese saved you
as their bombardment
sent the Pol Pot army fleeing.
But again, one by one,
your children left:
one killed by Khmer Rouge
one a refugee in a Thailand camp
and three off to the United States.

One son was missing.

In spite of hunger
you kept living,
chanting prayers,
calling upon your dead husband,
invoking your ancestors, your deity
to pour rain on the earth,
to stop the war and stop others
from disarranging your home,
rearranging your fate,
and deranging your children.

Oh mother, I am grateful
for your sorrowful strength,
for your woman's instinct
to preserve life,
and for the dignity of your womb.
When you left us

two daughters remained at your side,
and the grandchildren you knew
starved to death.
The ones you never met
wished for your presence.

Now waiting is all I can do
to lay flowers on your grave,
to say goodbye,
to embrace you one last time,
to present myself to you
and show you how I am,

your son.

FATHER, WHY DID YOU COME?

You came with an army.
You came from Phnom Penh—
that monarchical place
of shining pagodas and palaces,
of France's colonial remains
smelling of money
and foreign perfume.

You studied at University,
you won political debates.
Your family was full of riches, wealth,
and all you could have to make you happy.
Yet you abandoned your parents,
your friends, and your education
to have eight children with a peasant woman
in this thatched-roof house.

I see you marrying my mother,
vowing to plow the rice fields
like a peasant,
toiling in the sun
away from city life.
You enjoyed the things you earned:
the trust and love of friends,
and idle hours of sexual banter.

I see you carrying us
on your shoulders in front of the house,

playing galloping horse,
to make us hold on to you
forever.
Securing us with your eyes
when you stopped to reclaim your breath,
saying that you'd never leave us.

But you joined Lon Nol and the Americans
to fight the Vietcong.

I see you parting from us one by one,
while mother stood last in line
to be embraced,
with those same trusting eyes of affection.
"Papa will come back soon," you said,
while letting go of me
as I wished to climb on your shoulders.
Mother trembled in response,
"Come back to your children,
Come back and tell them why you left."

Months of letters went by
while radio newscasts about the war
confirmed the strength
of the Khmer Rouge army.
And one evening
a letter pronounced you dead.

A Vietcong had shot you.

Your sons banged their heads against trees
and all sought to avenge you.

Friends and neighbors gathered before the house,
while Mother wept
and your daughters surrounded her.

Oh, why did you come, father?
Why did you come?

A LETTER TO MY BROTHER

Lon Nol gave you a gun
but not a battle to fight.
You beat up your wife
for the love of whores.
Mother protested,
but soldiering
without a cause
had driven you mad.

You didn't think
I knew who you were,
The way you tortured your wife,
drove her nearly insane.
She took poison,
cut her wrist,
but she did not die.
I grew as a witness
to the tears she shed.

I imagined you with other women,
two or three at a time:
how you paid them to fight over you,
their manicured, painted nails
sharpened to pleasure
made you feel like a man;
how your fly unzipped for them
though your wife had tried
to push a dagger in her chest.

❋

You bemoaned her childlessness
in the form of blood
resembling your sons,
but you did not think of
the syphilis you brought home
with your lies and your cheating.

I survived your beating
when I stole your fried chicken
because I was hungry.
And now, in America, I remember
the way you dragged my sister-in-law
by the hair across the floor,
kicked me in the head with your boots,
threw me against the wall,
and allowed your drunken friend
to slap my face.

My voice fleeing my body,
I crouched and shivered
like a sick dog,
like a broken-winged bird.
I fluttered for air,
for my mother's arms.
I wanted to die.
Tears numbed my skull,
the weight of sorrow
like stones on my head.

April 17, 1975, spilled new year's blood
to end your reign over your wife
when the Khmer Rouge arrived.

They came in black pajamas,
checkered, red kramas around their heads,
looking for Lon Nol soldiers to execute
and scorching your brothel.

To survive you repressed
your sexual appetite,
nodding to every Khmer Rouge command.
Your calloused hands plowed
the land to seed rice,
your eyes closed to human feces
you carried to fertilize the fields
for one porridge meal each day.

And during the Khmer Rouge
you crawled back
to the arms of your wife,
pleading her for love
and understanding.
Rescued from the bruising of your fist,
she did not turn you in
for the crimes you had committed
against her.
She could inform the Khmer Rouge
that you spoke French,
the language of the colonists,
that you were a soldier of Lon Nol,
puppet of the American imperialists.

But she concealed your past
and protected you.

You survived
when the Vietnamese came,

but to free yourself
you decided to flee—
you, me, and sister, too—
all three to Thailand and then to America,
not knowing what
so far from home.

That night we crossed the border.
I stayed fanning mosquitoes
so you could dream in peace,
thinking of women
you licked and sniffed,
the eyes of whores loving you,
their breasts
anchoring you like pillows.

Then the thieves began shooting.
Without shoes, without warmth,
I ran past bushes of thorns
scraping my skin.
I was lost and alone,
teeth chattering from fear.
You were gone.
My sister was gone.
Everyone scattered in the dark.

I kept praying and talking to mother
on the other side of the world.
By luck, you came,
our sister came,
and the three of us slept in the cold
under dripping bamboo bushes,
hugging each other
afraid to let go.

You would not answer Thai thieves
telling us to surrender
while they searched for us
in the dark.
The red-eyed Thai bats
flew away to suck the blood
of other fleeing Cambodians,
and took the captured people
with them into the night.

In the morning we reached the camp.
We arrived safely,
though my body was full of wounds.
We fled across the border,
the three of us—
sister and brothers—
holding hands in the dark,
seeing hope in the sunrise.

Then again,
I hear your angry voice:
a deadly threat from man to boy.
Your eyes pierced my skin.
you made me crawl
and beg you to stop,
My screeching voice full of fear,
my gritted teeth full of hate.
my shirt tear-soaked.
I pissed in my pants as you beat me.

I didn't know how to forgive you.

I am older now.
I have put you away,
shed you from my mind.
You are no longer my nightmare.
I see you while
I soar among stars
in honor of mother's spirit,
whispering love and
wisdom of forgiveness
Because you are still my brother.

TO MY BROTHER THAI

You,
father of four
and fourth oldest,
slept that night
on a bamboo bed
under guava trees
beneath the star-filled sky.

Your brother feared
that you would infect
his children
if he let you inside
his thatched house.
So he put you outside
to die in your loneliness,
filled with yearnings
and prayers
for another chance at life.

Your eyes stayed open
for your children and wife
in America,
and for the prostitutes
with whom you'd slept.
Rampant in your disease,
your brain flooded with remorse
for what
you could have been.

A LETTER TO MY SISTER, SARATH

I think of you at home,
in Colorado,
watching late hour movies
with your husband and children,
visiting with Cambodians
who talk behind your back.
I think of the distance
between us, America
and our childhood in Cambodia.

I remember the aroma of rice
wrapped in banana leaves,
our mother's fried fish
dipped and soaked in pig's fat.
Her tamarind, shrimp paste
made our mouths water.
Our stomachs growled in hunger.

And sometimes in memory I weep,
pacing the steps of our journey
through rice paddies
in the gray mist of dawn;
how mornings we'd walk the same path
hearing frogs croaking,
birds chirping,
dogs howling,
water falling,
and the wind
jostling leaves of tall trees.

You carried a fishing net,
I carried a bucket.
We ran tagging and skipping,
we sang, laughed, and quarreled.
And we forgot how hungry
and gaunt we had become.

When we reached the stream
I'd refuse to set foot in the icy water.
But your totalitarian will
would force me into it.
You did not waste time.
I hated your harsh voice,
the barbarism in your eyes
the sound of your knuckles
striking my skull.

At day's end our bucket was always
full of fish and shrimp,
more than we could carry.
We could have waited
for the temperature to rise,
but you kept insisting.
I would despise you
and pity you with compassion,
but love you as my protector,
my sister.

I cannot fathom that
we survived
bombs and bullets crisscrossing
the sky, day and night;
the Khmer Rouge starving us,

making us sleep in the rain,
working us to death
away from our mother,
brothers and sisters.

You pulled leeches from my legs,
fought boys who called me names.
laughed when I cried,
and gave me an equal part
to mother's rice.
And now you work
assembling life into dollars
one hour at a time
in a factory to pay bills.

You fold clothes into squares
on weekends at the Laundromat
You shop in malls
full of wealth and glitter,
and think of poor siblings
in Cambodia
pleading on tapes for money
you don't have.

And the Khmer Rouge's souvenirs
of torture and killing
are stored in the capital's museum.
There are blindfolded skulls
and broken bones stacked
as history books for your children
to read
and interpret.

I often think about our thatched house
and the country we abandoned:
exploding landmines,
dire poverty,
rape, robbery, and
murder of the thousands.
Our Cambodia wrapped in bandages,
Our mother's grave growing weeds.

I wonder what they have done
to those bricked buildings
full of bullet holes.
And I keep asking,
"How are the brothers and sisters
we left behind?"

TUOL SLENG

This place used to be my school.
This very room is where I sat
dreaming about a girl I knew.

But this very room had been turned
into small prison cells
to keep humans caged in:
Brick walls with bare windows
letting light in just slightly,
and a hole where crumbs
could be shoved to the dying.
A hole for imagining
an escape,
that this was all a bad dream.

Whose sons and daughters
were these faces on the wall?
Whose mothers and fathers
were being interrogated?
The children…
what crime did they commit?

I picture where they were,
how each was chained
to a metal bed.
I walk from one torture chamber
to another
deciphering the torture tools
and where the photographer stood
to capture the anguish,

the pain,
the blood of another's death.

I hear them screaming.

In one of the paintings on the wall
a baby is thrown in the air
and bayoneted,
skewered like a chicken on the spit.
The mother screams
while dragged by her hair,
her head banging
against a coconut tree.

This used to be my classroom,
where I sat in fear of my teacher
and thought about a girl.
Could that girl be here
in one of the photographs?
Was she one of those
shoved into a mass grave?
Was she raped, tortured,
burned, or buried alive?

Who among those school children
survived to tell the story?

A LETTER TO DEATH

An enemy's bullet entered his mouth
and lodged in his brain.
My father fell in your arms,
Death.

Old women in white—
the bald-headed grand nuns—
sit with feet folded and hands clasped
humbled in prayers.

Auntie was fortunate to encounter you
before They arrived.
She didn't have to experience
starvation and the prosecution of others.
For this, I am grateful.
Mother gave her a ceremony,
a ritual to appease the journey of the soul.
We covered her with pure white sheets.
We washed her hands and feet
with blessed holy water.

The Khmer Rouge did not have a religion.
They desecrated temples
and killed monks.
No one was allowed to have
a burial ritual for the dead.

During the Khmer Rouge
my stepfather became yours
with a swollen belly—

starvation.
No ceremonial arrangement or goodbye for him.
We wrapped up his body and dumped it
into a small ditch we dug up
on a hill with thousands of others.
The grass covers all.

My oldest brother was dragged
into a field one night for questioning.
They tied his hands behind his back
and beat him until you had taken him.
You greeted his mother-in-law, wife,
and two children from starvation.

The monks chant for the dead
and the mourners.
Groaning voices sting the walls,
escape the thatched roof,
and incense permeates our clothes.

My brother-in-law's death
has been videotaped.
I can watch it as if I'm there.
The dirty-faced children wander in sorrow
while men hammer the casket together.
The cameraperson focuses
on my sister's rage,
her scream shaking her husband's dead body,
hoping to wake him from sleep.
Her children want to take her hand
and lead her to a different place.

In a dream I see

my oldest brother and his family
with my mother.
"Are you here to take mother with you?"
He nods, turns his face,
And disappears.
My sister-in-law carries one of her children.
She does not say a word or look at me.
The faces of my living siblings appear
floating all around my mother's body.
They all look down.
Then I see my father enter the room
as a young man surrounded in radiance.
"Your're here for mother, too?," I ask.
He smiles.
"Yes, my son. I've come
to take your mother home."

With all of those others
once we were a family,
but they are gone and you remain.
I've tried to shun you,
Death,
to drive you away,
forgetting that you alone
can be depended on.

When I pick up a child,
I feel your hand pressed against mine
and remember that this child
is also yours.
When I pet my cat, I feel your breath on his fur.
In every blossom, I inhale your fragrance.
When I look into the mirror I find you there,

applying the somber cosmetics of age or sickness,
making me ready for the final entrance.

You remind me to live with every breath,
though life seems too cold at times to grasp,
too intangible and meaningless to comprehend.
But perhaps, dear Death, you have the answer.
Perhaps you hold secrets
to a life well spent.

BROTHER-IN-LAW

He learned to smoke
when he held a gun
in Vietnam, defending Saigon
with the Americans.

He's Kampuchea Krom
with Vietnamese eyes.
Married to a Khmer woman,
he has four children
and lives in his dream
home in Rhode Island.

Smoking two cartons
of cigarettes each week,
drinking two packs
of beer through morning and night,
friends and foes
have sat by his side.

But he remains alone:
smoking,
drinking,
shaping,
refining
his past through dreamy eyes.

ABOUT MY YOUNGEST SISTER

My sister has frail, delicate eyes,
a fragmented soul,
a two-way smile,
a side that's dark and unconsoled.
There's no joy in her being,
no light in her soul,
no radiance in her spirit,
no smile on her face.
She travels on curved, twisted realities
engineered by pain and sadness,
running into barbed wire
fences of tears
and concrete walls of despair
like a rubber ball
of sorrow and pain
that bounces back and forth.

She is the youngest to bear
the legacy of her siblings'
abuse and control.
I have no desire to become
another tyrant over her,
and I want to break free
of her violence and screams.
But sometimes her controlling impulses
demand that I embrace her need,
and bring forth my anger
and my threats.

We live in one room
on the 9th floor, she and I;
and my sister blames me
for bringing her here,
as though I had coerced her
to come with me to America.
I wish things could be different,
but this is fate:
every drop of my blood
is tied to her sorrow,
her grief,
and the memories of injustices
she encountered as a child.

She remains solid
in her resistance,
in her vicious rage
and senseless hatred
against her own people,
who she feels are responsible
for her miseries.
She wants nothing to do
with Cambodians in America.
She does not want to be
vulnerable to their gossip,
their spreading of lies about her.
What she says might be used against her.
They might tear her clothes,
Or spread her open and prick her
with their sharp, foul tongues.

To her it's black or white,
Light or dark,

From one extreme to the next.
So she prefers a hermit's life
to a gregarious one,
with her secrets sealed,
her life closed,
her thoughts and feelings reserved
and kept at a distance.

I sometimes breathe uneasily
with her in my eyes.
I want to liberate her
to be an American who is confident,
to be a woman in her own right,
under my shadow as her protector:
brother angel granting her wings
to soar wherever she pleases.
Because through it all
she is all that I have,
and the worst is resolved
by our need to be
in each other's life.

THE STORY MY GRANDMOTHER CANNOT TELL

In America,
Grandmother mourns her fate
trapped inside
a narrow high-rise apartment
in the Tenderloin of San Francisco.
She looks to her past
where there's nothing
but suffering and pain.
She looks to the future
where there isn't much either.

I often wonder what
she must be going through
in her mind.

She is home, during peacetime
with her friends and neighbors,
gathering legends and memories
of things long gone,
missing her green rice fields
before the harvest is gold,
thinking of the monsoon
dancing to her lullaby.
Salt in her Cambodian rainfall
drips to the ground,
down the canals and streams
of her memory.

In her homeland
people die
everyday without justice.
The bickering faces of her people
are still at war.
Political atrocities staged
made her a witness
to the death of those she loved.

She had a daughter
raped by boys with guns
pointed to her breasts.
Her husband was taken
in the middle of the night
to be tortured and shot.
This was what they did
to old men who wore glasses,
to young women with an intellect,
to children with clean hands,
and to people who prayed.

Now,
in the America
she thought was a paradise,
Grandmother sits
fenced in by fear
that one day her children
and grandchildren
will leave her,
spitting English in her face,
their broken Khmer torturing her.

They have become too American,
too modern to see

that she's too old and fragile
to talk back;
too slow to react
because she forgets.
She cannot change their minds.
She can only hold on
to the good in her past
and the hope
that someone will come along
to hear the bad.

I am the answer to her solitude.
I climb the stairs
to pay my visit.
Though not her real grandson,
we are connected
by our suffering and flight.
Words are not necessary.
We understand eyes and silence.

THE SECOND DAY: REUNION

Toward the end of my first month
in Cambodia,
I went to my old village
to help dig up the bones
of my brother-in-law and mother.
We carried their ashes through the streets
in a ceremonial procession,
and gave them a proper burial,
laying their souls to rest
in the Buddhist temple.

My brother-in-law had been buried
for a year since the day
he was shot by a thief.
One bullet in the chest,
and one in the jaw
from the mouth through the head,
just like my father who was shot
during the war.
My oldest sister,
now a widow with four children.

My sister is coming to me
with a dagger pointing to her past,
her fists motioning in search of walls.
I am ready for her scream
while she's hammering my brain
with her sorrowful stories.
Her dead husband rises with her every tomorrow.

She ponders the violence,
the sudden death of the man she loves,
how a gun was triggered,
shattering the temple of her Beloved's soul,
her only protector and security.

My brother is coming to me
for dollars to shower his women
with alcohol and cigarettes;
to feel powerful over his wounds,
over the eyes of mother's ghost
widening its dead stare.
He desires to crawl in the arms of his wife,
to be with his children in the United States,
and to wake up one morning
knowing that his body is free of HIV.

The malnourished hands
of my nieces and nephews
are coming for my attention,
their baby grins watering my distress.
I hear the rapid beat of their hearts,
I see their fatherless smiles,
their faces disfiguring my sunshine.

The Khmer Rouge are still coming
with torches to burn houses
and landmines to blow up bridges.
They come to rob villagers
of their peace,
their sanity,
and their hope.
They want to recruit orphans;

and the widows
with their bastards and belongings
are fleeing,
running from the possibility of death.

How do I explain and describe
this Cambodia,
this land without toys,
without childhood?
A land of sorrow
invading the eyes of the innocent,
in the fields of dirt
where children dance
to the sound of a never-ending war?

They remember chopped-up bodies,
they still think about blood:
how cheap it was to drain from a person,
how delightful it was to the killer.
When they sleep,
they dream of running,
panting like dogs to get away
from the knife
or the ax
or the gun,
with hatred aimed at them
wanting their breath to stop—
to take even their silence.

But they will return to their roots—
to those burned villages—
to rebuild their homes,
to replant their vegetables and rice.

They will go on laboring,
even in the peril of landmines,
procreating others to take their place
when they're gone.
Nothing will stop their will to live,
not even the Khmer Rouge.

ABOUT AUNT SAREY

Aunt Sarey's husband left her
for another woman
who was her best friend.
She has five children.
She doesn't know what to do
with her pain.

She must think of her children
while dreaming of water lilies,
the joy of her virgin years,
her innocence and beauty
that stirred the eyes
and hearts of men,
holding them captive.

Why would this man leave her?
What does this woman have
that I don't?
Did he ever love his children?
She blames herself for his weakness,
and doesn't want to believe
the answer to this last question,
because he wouldn't leave
if he did.

The memory:
Five years with the Khmer Rouge.
Recalling their shared struggle,
she cries, remembering:

their escape to Thailand,
the harshness of their survival
in the refugee camp,
Khao-I-Dang.
They were contained within
barbed wire fences,
with Thai soldiers
keeping close surveillance
while they escaped the bullets
of warring factions.

The future:
How can she live free of him
and the memories of her past?
They shared hunger,
hopes, and dreams,
the promised future
in America.

The reality:
A welfare mother,
she has no work skills.
She can not speak English
and lives in a large, lonely city
in America.
She is in San Francisco.
She is in Lowell.
She is in Stockton, Long Beach,
Revere, Boston,
And Lynn.

The choice:
The shattered glass of time

has been strewn as splinters
on the path of roses
that her love
spread before her.
She doesn't have the strength
to winnow away the deceit,
but she must
think of her children.

It takes a strong mother
to give light
to her innocent babies.
They must know
the signs of each season,
where and when
to put seeds in the ground.
They must know
where to lay their anger,
how to cure the pain.

She will teach them
Through a mirror of silence.

THE MEKONG RIVER

I've never been to the Mekong
but I've heard it cries
when blood spills on its bank,
when dismembered bodies
wash up on its shore
or when drowned eyeballs,
nipped by fish, come floating up.

Is it still the Nile of Life
or the Ganges of Purity and Healing?

By now, it must be choked
with rotten war planes, shrapnel
and bones of people deprived of voice,
dark people with vision skewed toward survival,
farmers still dying from those chemicals
the U.S. sprayed on their land.
Those bomb craters came like wounds,
in fury exploding souls.

Among Vietnam, Cambodia and Laos
are enough tears to fill the congested Mekong,
with the yearning and loss
of a few more generations to come.
There's no stopping.
They will continue to hope,
and this hope will float on tears.

REUNION

From the womb of life to death I shall return
To the majesty of my mother's presence
in the here of eternal peace,
I will know the joy of childhood again.

Her ancestral warriors shall lead me back to where I belong,
to the land of my birth,
in the milk of rice and wine of palms,
to the memory of a thatched-roof house full of strong women
raising their fists against the massacre of their innocence.

I, a child in the body of a man,
think of loved ones I never got to know.
But I shall dance for them in the monsoon's cleansing rain,
my mother's embrace uniting us all.

Having known her is my sorrow and my inheritance.

www.ingramcontent.com/pod-product-compliance
Lightning Source LLC
Chambersburg PA
CBHW021914040426
42447CB00007B/848